50 AMAZING
PLACES IN CHINA

TITLES IN THE SERIES

Chinese Ceramics
JI WEI

Chinese Characters
NINA TRAIN CHOA

Chinese Calligraphy
ZHOU KEXI

Chinese Painting
DENG MING

Chinese Tea
LING YUN

50 Amazing Places in China
DONG HUAI

56 Ethnic Groups in China
DAI DUNBANG

Famous Flowers in China
QIAN XINGJIAN

Chinese Motifs of Good Fortune
LIU SHENGHUI & ZHU WEN

Chinese Architecture
WANG QIJUN

Contemporary Architecture in China
ARCHITECTURAL CREATION MAGAZINE

The Giant Panda
FANG MIN

Discovering China

50 AMAZING
PLACES IN CHINA

Better Link Press

This book is edited and designed by the Editorial Committee of *Cultural China* series

Managing Directors: Wang Youbu, Xu Naiqing
Editorial Director: Wu Ying
Editors: Ye Jiasheng, Anna Nguyen
Editorial Assistants: Xu Xiaoyin, Li Mengyao

Text by Dong Huai
Images by Quanjing, Phototime
Cover Image: Getty Images

Cover Design: Wang Wei
Interior Design: Yuan Yinchang, Li Jing, Hu Bin

ISBN: 978-1-60220-122-4

Address any comments about *Discovering China: 50 Amazing Places in China* to:

Better Link Press
99 Park Ave
New York, NY 10016
USA
or
Shanghai Press and Publishing Development Company
F 7 Donghu Road, Shanghai, China (200031)
Email: comments_betterlinkpress@hotmail.com

Printed in China by Shenzhen Donnelley Printing Co., Ltd.

3   5   7   9   10   8   6   4

CONTENTS

Preface..............9

1. THE NORTHERN REGION 11

Mohe 14

Sky Lake of Changbai Mountain 16

Imperial Summer Mountain Resort 20

The Great Wall 24

The Forbidden City 30

The Summer Palace 33

Temple of Heaven 37

Yuanmingyuan Park 40

Shichahai 42

Yungang Caves 45

Pingyao City 50

Hukou Waterfalls 52

Terra-cotta Army 54

2. THE WESTERN REGION 57

Mogao Grottoes 59

Mingsha Hills and Crescent Moon Spring 64

Emei Mountain 66

CONTENTS

Jiuzhai Valley 68

Huanglong Gully 70

Hailuogou 73

Hanas Lake 76

Potala Palace 78

Nam Co 82

Mount Qomolangma 84

3. THE CENTRAL REGION 87

Qufu 90

Longmen Caves 94

Yellow Mountain 98

Hong Village and Xidi Village 102

Slender West Lake 104

Suzhou Gardens 106

Three Gorges 110

Fenghuang City 113

Zhangjiajie 116

West Lake 118

CONTENTS

Lu Mountain 120
Wuyuan 122
The Bund in Shanghai 124

4. THE SOUTHERN REGION 127
Shangri-La 129
Meili Snow Mountain 132
Lijiang 134
Lugu Lake 136
Yellow Fruit Tree Waterfall 138
Yuanyang Terraced Fields 140
Li River 142
Yangshuo 144
World's End in Hainan Island 146
Hakka Earth Towers 148
Xiamen Gulangyu 150
Sun Moon Lake 152
Hong Kong Victoria Harbor 154
Macau 156

PREFACE

What is the most beautiful place in China? With such a broad question, we can hardly give a satisfactory answer. It is impossible to provide a short list because China's geographical features and rich traditions vary greatly from south to north, and from west to east. It's difficult to directly compare all the beautiful and fascinating places in China. Each place has its unique lure and striking qualities.

However, we try to depict not a all-encompassing China, but rather a representation of its striking beauty. Therefore, we carefully selected the most well-known scenic spots from the World Heritage list, with 5A level tourist attractions appraised by China National Tourism Administration, and the best geography places voted by the *Chinese National Geography*—a professional geographical magazine. We want to unfold a magnificent landscape of mountains, rivers and human treasures, in order for readers to experience the diversified vistas of China achieved by nature through thousand-of-years.

THE NORTHERN REGION

Strictly speaking, this region refers to the areas that include the northeast (Heilongjiang, Jilin, Liaoning provinces); Inner Mongolia Autonomous Region; Hebei, Shanxi, and Shaanxi provinces as well as Beijing, Tianjin municipalities.

The northeast area is the cradle of the Manchus, who established what was to become the last of China's imperial dynasties. The region is bounded to the north, east and southeast by four main rivers—the Heilongjiang, Wusulijiang, Tumenjiang and Yalujiang—and within the territories that they form there are four principal mountain ranges: the Qian, Changbai, Da Xing'an (Hinggan) Ling and Xiao Xing'an (Hinggan) Ling.

Of these, Changbai offers the most dramatic scenery. Its main peak, Baitou, the tallest in the northeast, is capped with snow all year round, and on its upper slopes lies the beautiful and moody Sky Lake (*tian chi*)—a huge volcanic crater-lake surrounded by 16 precipitous mountain peaks. The lake's waters can be beautifully serene one day, and change the next day to a maelstrom of high winds and crashing waves.

The Changbai Range is also the source of another important river in the northeast, the Songhuajiang, the main tributary of the Heilongjiang. Winding through about 60

percent of the territory, the Songhuajiang feeds two of the most attractive cities of the area—Jilin, the "river city," and Harbin. Jilin is famous for its frozen "tree hangings" in winter months. Harbin (one of the origins of its name is said to be a combination of a Manchu phrase for "honor" and "great reputation") is celebrated for its beautiful Spring Festival, when the streets are lit at night with ice lanterns, and ice and snow sculptures are displayed in its parks.

The northern region offers a history that is just as rich in its ancient cities and cultural landmarks—its imperial cities, the nation's seats of power at various times in the vast span of more than two thousand years from the early Warring States to the collapse of the Qing as either dynastic strongholds or imperial capitals, which are dominated by the majesty and grandeur of Beijing's Forbidden City, the home of 24 Chinese emperors in the Ming and Qing dynasties; its temples, monasteries and other religious monuments, most notably in the city of Xi'an, where the terra-cotta army of the first Qin emperor, considered the father of Chinese unity, stands guard over the souls of China's imperial past among other relics.

The Yellow River Basin in the central part of the northern region is the site of one of the most important archaeological discoveries of all time—the skull of the Peking Man, unearthed at Zhoukoudian in Hebei Province. Scientists regard it as the evidence of human existence along the river flats more than half a million years ago.

It is a region immensely rich not only in history, but also in natural resources. The soil is largely soft loess and exceptionally fertile. It encompasses the north end of the Grand Canal, the world's greatest man-made waterway. The waters of the mighty Yellow River, Hai River and Yangtze River are linked and harnessed by the canal. The monumental waterway was built over a period of more than 2000 years between Hangzhou, a renowned city in the central region, and Tianjin to support vast croplands of wheat, cotton, corn, sorghum, peanuts, tobacco and soybeans. It also provided an efficient and relatively inexpensive inland transport system for agricultural products and the region's large deposits of coal, iron ore, and salt.

Mohe

This, the northernmost outpost of China, is called the Arctic City because of its bitterly cold winter climate. Its people call it the town of the White Night for the time of the annual summer solstice, when darkness closes in for only an hour or two before and after midnight. But its most dramatic feature is its natural son et lumière of the aurora borealis, the northern lights, when a small ring of light appears to the north of the city, expands until it literally fills the sky with color, then retreats and disappears to the east.

Mohe is called the Arctic City because of its bitterly cold winter climate.

Sky Lake of Changbai Mountain

This huge volcanic mountain range, stretching from southeast Jilin Province to the northern part of the Korean Peninsula, is one of the great natural treasures of China. It is rich in beauty, abounds with exotic wildlife and is a major source of ingredients for one of the most complex and most valued instructions of Chinese culture—herbal medicine. Chinese historians attribute the birth of Chinese medicine to a legendary emperor, Shen Nong Shi, who is said to have reigned some 5000 years ago and to have become fascinated by the apparent medicinal properties of various plants. "Shen Nong Shi tested the myriad herbs," wrote the Han dynasty historian Sima Qian (Ssuma Chien), "and so the art of medicine was born." That art has developed over the centuries into an immense pharmacopoeia of potions, pills, salves, tonics and other remedies taken from plants or from animals and reptiles.

Millions of years ago the Changbai Mountain (Snow capped Mountains) thundered and rocked with almost continuous volcanic eruptions. The legacy of that prehistoric violence is a series of 60 deep craters that have since filled with water to form the beautiful and brooding Sky Lake, south of Baihe County in Jilin Province. It is one of the world's most magnificent sights, lying just over 6560 ft (2000 m) above sea level, covering an area of 3.55 sq. mi. (9.2 sq. km). Its waters are more than 984 ft (300 m) deep in some places and surrounded by 16 mountains peaks.

Changbai Mountain was once an active volcano, and although it has erupted twice in relatively modern times—in the 17th and 18th centuries—it is now considered dormant. It features a group of 72 lakes, which were formed from volcanic craters, the largest being the spectacular Sky Lake (*tian chi* in Chinese).

In fine weather, you can see the rocks at the bottom of the lake's bed because of the serene and clear waters. But the weather can change creating endless 3-ft (1-m) high waves on the lake. In the winter months, the lake freezes, mirroring the mountain peaks around it.

Imperial Summer Mountain Resort

The Imperial Summer Mountain Resort in Chengde, the biggest garden palace complex in China, was started in 1703 and took 87 years to complete. It was a summer resort for the Qing emperors and was also known as the Jehol Traveling Lodge or Li Palace. Its grounds, only 20 percent of which are lakes and gardens, and the rest hills, are guarded by a wall that runs 6.2 mi. (10 km) around the perimeter.

The Resort itself includes the Central Palace, Pine-and-Crane Studio, East Palace and a residential complex known as Wan He Song Feng. As with all Chinese courts, the architecture is elegant with one aim in mind: to promote peace and harmony. Bronze lions guard the outer gate, and the main door to the compound proclaims its name in characters that are said to have been inscribed by Emperor Kangxi himself. Visitors can view the Dan Bo Jing Cheng ceremonial hall, built of *nanmu* (cedar), the emperor's bedchamber and a two-story mansion in which the stairs form part of an artificial hill of rock.

There are a lot of interesting spots inside. For example, Misty Rain Mansion, as its name suggests, was specially designed for the enjoyment of mist and rain on the surrounding lakes and hills. Standing on the rise of Great Lotus Island, it is a two-story single-eaved building supported by red pillars and clad with green glazed

The décor of the entire palace complex is pleasantly free of ornate carvings, gilt or decorative paintings—a pure rustic from summer dust storms and the political heat of court life in Beijing.

tiles. Its name was bestowed by Emperor Kangxi, and it is inscribed in his own hand on a plaque on the upper floor.

The Zhijingyun Dyke, a vast and beautiful series of pools and water gardens modeled on the West Lake of Hangzhou, was laid in one of 36 scenic spots selected by the Emperor Kangxi.

The Heavy-Snow-on-South-Hill Pavilion, with its winged tentlike roof, was given its name by Kangxi and stands rather precariously on the edge of a bluff.

Shuixin (Lake Center) Pavilion, lying north of the main palace area and south of Misty Rain Mansion, was once the Watergate on the border of the lakes.

Built in 1767, the lamasery Putuo Zongcheng Temple is designed in a series of terraced steps up a broad hillside and is modeled on the seat of Tibetan Buddhism, the Potala Palace in Lhasa.

This statue, the Thousand Hands and Thousand Eyes Bodhisattva, one of the biggest wooden Buddha images on the world, stands more than 72 ft (22 m) high and is constructed of five different timbers: elm, fir, pine, juniper and cypress.

The lamasery Putuo Zongcheng Temple is in a series of terraced steps up a broad hillside.

The Great Wall

Long before the Great Wall itself was built, primitive defensive mounds and walls were thrown up here and there throughout northern China to protect tribal groups from surprise attack. According to ancient records, the state of Chu built walls in the 7th century BC in the areas that are now Henan and Hubei Provinces.

The Great Wall of the Warring States emerged from several defensive lines of tamped earth built by the various states, and it was these unconnected walls that were joined together and strengthened to form the first stage of the Great Wall in the Qin dynasty. The Qi wall was built in the 5th century BC in what is now the province of Shandong. It runs from Pingyin in the west, around the northern slopes of Tai Mountain, and ends at the coast.

When the first emperor of Qin dynasty ordered the linking up of older tribal walls, the Great Wall forced into labor some 500,000 peasants, among them many convicted criminals. In the later interim and unstable rule of the Northern Wei (AD 386–AD 534), another 300,000 people were put to work on a single section south of Datong. In AD 607–AD 608, when north-south political divisions were still shaking the foundations of Chinese unity, a full 1 million people were further called upon. But all this paled against the many millions of laborers conscripted during the Ming dynasty (1368–1644) to modernize, strengthen and extend the wall—this stage of the project alone took more than 100 years to complete.

Nothing can compare to the immense human labor that went into the construction, and almost constant renovation, and expansion of the greatest of monument to Chinese civilization: the Great Wall.

The result is nothing short of a human marvel, a man-made protective barrier that snakes a distance of 3728 mi. (6000 km) over and through the rumpled folds of the northern Chinese landscape from Shanhaiguan on the shores of the Bo Sea, through Hebei, Beijing, Shanxi, Inner Mongolia, Shaanxi, Ningxia and Gansu Provinces until it reaches Jiayuguan in the arid west. During each work campaign, thousands died of sickness, accident, exposure or simply the physical ordeal. Handcarts were used on flat land or gentle slopes, and goats and donkeys sometimes hauled the bricks and lime, but otherwise it was harsh and unremitting human toil that built this most spectacular man-made structure.

The Great Wall is a monument to the human spirit and a memorial to immeasurable human suffering.

Almost everything on the Great Wall was done by hand. Workers passed raw materials from one to another—rock, earth, bricks, lime and site—up mountainsides and along ridges to each worksite.

The Forbidden City

Better known all over the world as Beijing's Forbidden City, the Ancient Palaces were the residence and political nerve center of the emperors of the Ming and succeeding Qing dynasties. The original palaces, which took 15 years to build, were started in 1406 by the third emperor of the Ming dynasty, Zhu Di, when he moved the imperial capital to Beijing. The complex, the largest surviving cluster of wooden buildings on such a scale in the world, has since played a central role in the most momentous phases of modern Chinese history—the wealth, power and glory of the Ming, the Manchu triumph of the Qing dynasty (1644–1911), then its gradual decay in the face of foreign pressure and incursion, and finally the complete collapse of the dynastic order.

The Forbidden City is girdled by a 10-m-high city wall and a 52-m-wide moat. It measures 961 m long from north to south and 753 m wide from east to west, covering 780,000 sq. m. There is a gate on each side of the rectangular city wall. The layout of the architecture's complex within the city all centers on the north-south axis and sprawls eastward and westward. The architecture's red walls, golden glazed tiles, engraved beams, painted rafters rival in magnificence.

The Forbidden City was so called because the common people were forbidden to enter it, and observation and security towers placed at each corner of the 1.6-million-sq. ft (150,000-sq.-m)

After the fall of the Manchus and establishment of the short-lived Chinese republic, the Forbidden City fell into disrepair, but was restored in the 1950s, according to its original plans. The spirits of 24 great and not-so-great divine rulers of China's immense past still face south, according to ancient Chinese geomancy, and their people face north in obedience.

palace grounds made certain that all but the aristocracy were kept out.

Palace of Heavenly Purity, as Qing dynasty reception and banqueting hall also served a crucial role in the security and harmony of the dynastic order. It was where the Qing emperors chose their successors. From the time of Emperor Yongzheng, who assumed the throne in 1723, it was the custom for each ruler to write the name of his intended successor on two pieces of paper —one to be kept in his personal possession and the other secreted behind a plaque bearing the inscription "Frank and Honest." Upon the emperor's death, his closest minister would compare the two names, and if they tallied, they announced the new ruler. More than 40 mansions surround the Palace of Heavenly Purity, some of them containing the emperor's crown and robes of office and books and artworks; other being places where he held audiences with his chief scholars and advisers; and still others being used as reading rooms, medical consulting rooms and living quarters for the imperial servants, maids, concubines and palace eunuchs.

The Palace Museum was founded in 1925 to oversee the protection of the existing relics and artifacts in the collections of the Forbidden City.

The Summer Palace

The powerful and ruthless Empress Dowager (Cixi), the last real dynastic ruler of China, built the Summer Palace in 1888 on the site of a previous palace and garden that had dated from the Jin dynasty (1115–1234).

The project has since been regarded as something of an extravagant folly. For one thing, the empress appropriated much of the cost of it, some 24 million taels of silver, from funds set up to modernize the Chinese navy—and was soon to see the navy, or fleets of magnificent but obsolete and outgunned war junks, suffer a humiliating defeat under the guns and rockets of British iron-hulled steam-paddle warship brought from England to smash open the doors to free trade in China.

Nowadays its lake, gardens, shrines and pavilions are open to the public, along with another symbol of the empress Dowager's stubborn extravagance, the giant Marble Boat on Kunming Lake, a stone replica of a showboat paddle steamer.

A bronze pavilion, called Pavilion of Precious Clouds, is another feature of the Summer Palace. It was cast in 1750 and reaches a height of nearly 26 ft (8 m) and weighs more than 200 tons.

Composed mainly of Longevity Hill and Kunming Lake, the Summer Palace occupies an area of 294 ha. A number of streams from the western districts of Beijing, including one called Jade

The Summer Palace had become a luxurious royal garden providing imperial families with rest and entertainment.

Allied Forces gutted and plundered the Summer Palace in 1860, and a subsequent rebuilding project only added to its great cost.

Spring Mountain, were channeled by engineers of the Yuan dynasty to form the great lake of the Summer Palace—the Kunming Lake. The Qing emperor, Qianlong, gave it its original name the Garden of Clear Ripples (Qingyi Yuan) when he refurbished a Ming dynasty palace and temple, the Duobao Pagoda, to celebrate his mother's 60th birthday. Later, the Empress Dowager added much of the rest of the construction around the lake, including the Palace Which Dispels Clouds, which she built to celebrate her own birthday.

Temple of Heaven

Tiantan, the Temple of Heaven, in the southwestern corner of Beijing, is an ensemble of shines and was once the venue for the most important imperial rite—prayers for good harvest, sacrifices to the gods and royal ancestors and communion with the heavens. The buildings are spaced out over an area of more than 29.4 million sq. ft (2,700,000 sq. m), and altogether took 14 years to build.

The Temple of Heaven consists of two main structures linked by an 1188-ft-long (360-m-long) bridge. It is regarded as the most remarkable architectural composition, in which mathematical balance and economy of design have achieved an almost overwhelming majesty. It is also a masterpiece of acoustics, its most novel feature being a circular wall of polished bricks in Huangqiong House (Imperial Vault of Heaven), where echoes run clearly from one end to another, giving it the name Echo Wall. This hall also contains sacred ancestral tablets, as well as those dedicated to the gods of rain, the sun, the moon, the stars, dawn, the wind, thunder and lightning. When Western troops invaded Beijing in 1860 and 1900, the Temple of Heaven suffered serious damage, and it was not until 1918 that the temple was repaired and reopened to the public.

Qiniandian is the Temple for Praying for a Good Harvest with a detail of its domed ceiling, dominates the Temple of Heaven from the top of three concentric terraces fenced with carved white marble balustrades. Qiniandian is where the emperor came each year at the first full moon for fertility rites that go back to the distant beginnings of Chinese history. At the winter solstice he would also mount the three terraces of the Circular Sacrificial Altar where, after much prayer and traditional clay pipe music, a young bullock would be sacrificed to the gods. As such, the emperor was the vital conduit between the teeming Chinese society and the spiritual forces that ruled much of its existence.

Built in 1420 (the 18th year of the reign of the Ming emperor Yongle), the Temple of Heaven is part of a series of four temples in Beijing representing the firmament. The others are the Temple of the Sun, the Temple of the Earth, and the Temple of the Moon.

Yuanmingyuan Park

The ruins of Yuanmingyuan Park, the imperial gardens of the Summer Palace outside Beijing, are still a famous destination in China even though few traces of its magnificent beauty remain today. For over 150 years the gardens, bridges, pagodas and residences were the pet project of emperors who based their design on well-known scenic spots in China and other famous garden designs. The area for the gardens was already blessed with an abundance of natural springs and hills, but that was just the raw material for the creation of a fairytale landscape that exemplified the imperial desire to have all the beauty of China belong within the emperor's garden walls. Rivers, waterfalls, lakes and islands dotted the transformed landscape. The theme of each special garden site was created to represent China's cherished artistic, literary and philosophical concepts that the emperor then had the privilege of naming. The finest materials went in to the building of the garden's exquisite architecture. These marvelous structures were furnished from the vast imperial collections of art, antiques and books. As contact with the West began to influence imperial taste, Western building and art objects were added to Yuanmingyuan Park. The gardens represented the culmination of 2000 years of Chinese garden design. It was razed to the ground by the Anglo-French Allied Forces in 1860. The weakened Qing dynasty in the second half of the 19th century was unable to protect China, and as foreign powers vied in Beijing for the rich spoils, the imperial gardens were eventually set on fire and the treasures looted.

In the past, the gardens were the home of the emperor and his court from the beginning of each Chinese lunar New Year in early spring until autumn. For many years, even after being in a disastrous state of ruin, the gardens inspired poetry describing its tragic beauty.

Shichahai

Shichahai is a majestic lake located in Beijing downtown. It is an attractive sanctuary from the hustle and bustle of the day.

Walking around Shichahai inevitably provides a sense of its history. Ancient Shichahai was surrounded by 10 temples. *"cha"* refers to a small temple while *"shi"* means "ten," hence the name of Shichahai. It is composed of three man-made lakes: Qianhai ("Front Sea" Lake), Houhai ("Rear Sea" Lake) and Xihai ("West Sea" Lake). They once formed a part of a system of waterways that fed into the Imperial Capital. For centuries, wooden boats carrying produce from the south would make the journey up the Grand Canal and enter the city via these waterways. After a period of decline, the lakes then became a prime recreational destination. With overhanging willows lining its banks and café bars tucked away in its many secluded corners, it is wonderful to relax over a drink while taking in the tranquil atmosphere.

Ancient temples and lake, together with the grey-wall quadrangles, constitute the typical landscape of Shichahai. Amidst these quadrangles there a number of homes of former celebrities including Prince Gong's (the sixth son of Qing emperor Daoguang) Mansion.

The main scenes of Shichahai are the Beihai Park at the south end of Qianhai Lake, the magnificent Drum (Gulou) and Bell (Zhonglou) Towers which functioned as important timepieces of the

Shichahai is a peaceful island amid the sea of activity in the surrounding metropolis and provides a tranquil escape to stressed workers seeking a sense of space and well-being.

Imperial Capital from as early as the 15th century, and the elegant Wanning Bridge, constructed from marble only two years ago, standing above a canal, which once flowed to the south of the Old City.

As we leave Qianhai and reach Houhai, we spot the intricately decorated Silver Ingot Bridge crossing a canal leading from the lake. Once an area full of commercial activity, today it only overlooks the pleasure boats passing quietly underneath. Heading eastward is the Lane of the Long Stem Pipe Makers, a street whose earlier canal-related commercial function has also given way to more café bars. Ya Er Lane, opposite the lane, heads northwest. This narrow alley—away from the chaos around the bridge—offers a step back in time. Mostly lined with residential buildings, there are some fascinating structures, including an elaborate two-story white building that features a contrasting timber balcony.

Yungang Caves

The Yungang grottoes are located 10 mi. (16 km) west of Datong in Shanxi. Carved into the southern slope of Mount Wuzhou more than 1500 years ago, they are rated as one of the three most significant examples of Buddhist cave art in China. Ancient records indicate that the caves were situated close to a community of Buddhist monasteries flourishing in the Liao (AD 907–1125) and Jin (1115–1234) dynasties. There are now 53 caves in all, covering almost 0.6 mi. (1 km) of the cliff face and containing over 51,000 Buddhist images. Three different periods and styles of Buddhist art are represented. The central caves, the largest and earliest to be carved, contain images that are said to have been modeled on the rulers of the Northern Wei dynasty (AD 386–AD 534). Each of the five grottoes (numbers 16–20) contains a statue of Buddha at least 43 ft (13 m) tall. The one in grotto number 19 is the most imposing, while the gigantic Buddha sitting outside grotto number 20, with a dignified but faintly amused expression, is said to be carved in typical Northern Wei style.

Of all the grottoes in Yungang, Grottoes numbers 9 and 13 are noted for the ornate and brightly colored flower-and-plant motifs, altars, sculptured musicians and instruments added there by artists of the Qing dynasty. The most commanding relic of this section is a huge cross-legged Buddha, 43 ft (13 m) high, reposing in grotto number 13 and representing a sculptural style that is unique in Yungang. Between its right arm and thigh stands a much smaller statue of a "four-armed strongman."

Another grotto that has drawn a great deal of attention is grotto number 5. Linked to grotto number 6, which is the largest in Yungang, this grotto has a four-tiered wooden structure decorating its entrance.

Stupas of innumerable forms and variations are found in the eastern caves, while the western caves contain figures that bear the influence of Indian art.

Along with the Longmen Caves and the Mogao Grottoes, the Yungang Caves has been rated as one of the three most significant examples of Buddhist cave art in China.

Pingyao City

Pingyao City, historically one of the first cities in northern China, is famous as a walled city with many traditional dwellings, government offices, shops, and temples dating to the Ming and Qing dynasties that are still intact. Zhenguo Temple and Shuanglin Temple house painted statues dating from 400–1000 years old. It was established during the Western Zhou dynasty (c.1046 BC–c.711 BC), but the old city wall seen today was recent by comparison, built in 1370 during the Ming dynasty. There is a long-held belief in the area that the rammed earth and brick wall in the shape of a tortoise is key to the 2700-year history of Pingyao, since the tortoise is one of the symbols of longevity in Chinese culture. The city gates on the east and west sides are compared to the legs of the tortoise, and the south and north gates are the head and tail of the animal. Two wells outside the south gate are like the eyes, and the streets and lanes seem to suggest the pattern of the tortoise's shell.

At its prime, Pingyao City's strategic location on the banks of the Yellow River in Shanxi gave it power as a transportation hub and commercial center.

Hukou Waterfall

Subject of poetry, art and legend, Hukou Waterfall is the second largest falls in China, located on the Yellow River, between Ji County, Shanxi Province and Yichuan County, Shaanixi Provine. It has a various width from 30m to 50m and a fall of over 20m. As the river winds like a yellow dragon through Central China, it narrows and plunges through a gap. The water speeds up with increasing waterpower and rushes down from the narrow gap as if it is poured down from a huge teapot; hence ti is named Hukou (*hu*, kettle; *kou*, spout) waterfall. The yellow mists that rise high above the tumultuous water at the base of the fall have been called "smoke from the river" since on sunny days the yellow spray appears to turn gray and then blue, like smoke. The legendary hero Yu the Great of ancient China is said to have taken over the monumental task of controlling the flooding of the Yellow River from his father, who was killed for his arrogance at attempting to change this force of nature that is the Yellow River. Yu, instead, led the people to tunnel through mountains and cut through ridges to make a safe passage for the river.

This narrow space filled with the rushing river water suggests a teapot spout, which is the translation of the Chinese name for the falls.

Terra-cotta Army

The vast tomb of Emperor Qin Shihuang, the first Chinese emperor to unify China's warring clans 2000 years ago, might never have been discovered since its highly skilled designers had hidden it extremely well. There is some evidence that long ago grave robbers inadvertently set fires in their search for treasures, but the tomb commissioned by Emperor Qin Shihuang lay quietly 15 to 20 ft (4.5 to 6.5 m) below the Earth's surface, covered by a roof built with layers of fiber mats followed by many feet of soil to conceal it. There is speculation that the tombs workers and supervisors were buried alive at completion to protect its secrets. In 1974, peasants near Xi'an uncovered evidence of the tomb's fabulous terra-cotta army when digging a well. Their well excavation was over an area of the tomb with more than 8000 life-size terra-cotta warriors. The figures had been fired at higher than usual temperatures for terra-cotta and were shaped by using cleverly carved molds to allow for hollow torsos, heads and arms. The legs were solid terra-cotta needed to support each figure's overall weight of up to 600 lb (300 kg). Experts believe this terra-cotta army is only a small part of the buried treasures of Emperor Qin Shihuang's tomb since it lies approximately less than a mi. (1000 m) east of the main tomb. The main entrance to the tomb has still not been located even to this day.

The warriors' infinitely varied details of facial features, hair, dress, rank, and horses for cavalry divisions mean that no two are alike.

THE WESTERN REGION

The western region of China is an area of striking contrasts. It is arid, yet rich in life-giving water resources. It covers a vast area of about 1.5 million sq. mi. (4 million sq. km) that is flat, inhospitable and rated among the bleakest of the world's deserts—yet it also features massive snowcapped mountain ranges that roll like huge ocean waves into the Himalayas. It is an area of abundant resources—minerals, salt, oil, and forest products—yet it is also where China's aerospace centers can be found, the country's most advanced technology. It has always been regarded as the main defensive frontier of Chinese civilization, yet it was once the Middle Kingdom's only channel of communication with Central Asia, the Middle East and the rest of the world.

It is an area that embraces the Xinjiang Uygur Autonomous Region, Gansu, Qinghai, Ningxia Hui Autonomous Region, Sichuan, Chongqing Municipality and Tibet (Xizang Autonomous Region). It features the highest major river in the world, the Yarlung Zangbo (Yalu Tsangpo), with an average elevation of about 4,000 m, and one of the world's highest lakes, the Nam Co, with an elevation of 4718 m, which lies north of the Tibetan capital, Lhasa.

The Xinjiang Uygur Autonomous Region is divided by the Tianshan Range into two vast desert basins, the Tarim in the south and Junggar in the north. In the Tarim, there lies one of the two most dreaded deserts in China, and Taklimakan, an 309,000-sq. mi. (800,000-sq. km) stretch of 328-ft (100-m) high shifting dunes and fierce sandstorms. North of these basins lies the Gobi desert, the fifth largest in the world.

Mogao Grottoes

The Mogao Grottoes were cut into the precipitous eastern slope of Mingsha Mountain about 15 mi. (25 km) southeast of Dunhuang. The earliest grotto was built in 366 by the monk Le Zun, and more than a thousand others were added in the following centuries. By the year AD 698, the complex was already so well established that Li Huairang produced an account called "Renovating the Buddhist Shrines in Mogao Grottoes."

In 1900, a Taoist priest, Wang Yuanlu, opened up a sealed grotto and found some 50,000 Buddhist relics dating from the Jin (AD 265–AD 420) to Song (AD 960–1279) dynasties including scriptural texts, portraits, books, and embroideries.

Today only 492 grottoes remain, but they are packed with treasures—murals covering a total area of 53,820 sq. yd. (45,000 sq. m), 3400 bas-relief and three-dimensional wall sculptures, several thousand pillars with the lotus motif, and floral floor tiles and five ornate wooden shrines built in the Tang dynasty (AD 618 –AD 907).

The sculptural figures in the various caves are made of clay and painted, and they range in height from a few inches (centimeters) to 108 ft (33 m). The murals present a wide and colorful range of subjects, including gloomy and mysterious stories from the 5th to 7th centuries, exuberant and more refined paintings of the Buddhist scriptures from the period after the Sui dynasty (AD 581–AD 618) and two particular murals showing an ancient map of Wutai Mountain and the "journey of Zhan Yichao and his wife."

Some of China's greatest Buddhist art treasures are found in the Mogao Grottoes, or Thousand Buddha Caves.

The ancient artists and craftsmen at Dunhuang combined the styles from central China with those of western regions, creating Buddhist art work with Chinese characteristics.

Mingsha Hills and
Crescent Moon Spring

4 mi. (6 km) south of Dunhuang and close to the Crescent Moon oasis, the fierce winds of the desert have whipped the sands into a series of tall and dramatically shaped dunes called Mingsha Hills. Legend has also added to the drama of this strangely beautiful place. The name of the dunes translates as "murmuring sand," referring to a noise like distant thunder that comes from the action of the wind on the sail-like curves that it has sculptured in the dune's faces.

It is said that there was once a general who set up camp here on his way to the Western frontier. During the night, a violent sandstorm blew up and buries him along with his army. The "murmur" from the dunes is said to be the cries of the buried souls.

Crescent Moon Spring, this desert oasis lies among towering sand dunes about 4 mi. (7 km) south of Dunhuang. It is a small spring, only 328 ft (100 m) long and 82 ft (25 m) wide, but is fed so abundantly with subterranean water that it has never been known to dry up, even in the fiercest sandstorms.

Rushes grow around the water's edge, and there are trees on the east bank. In the spring the small lake becomes a popular visiting spot, especially at the time of the Dragon Boat Festival when pilgrimages are made to the nearby Mingsha Hill. The crescent-shaped spring is also noted for one of its inhabitants, the "iron-back" fish, and an herb called "seven star," both of which have health-giving properties and have thus provided the lake with the name Medical Spring.

As the *Dunhuang County Gazette* describes Crescent Moon Spring: "It is beautiful and unfathomably deep (and) remains clear, though threatened sometimes by tumultuous conditions of the surrounding dunes."

Emei Mountain

The Song dynasty poet Fan Chengda wrote of Emei Mountain:

The Great Emei stretches its arms in friendly welcome,
While Little Emei and Middle Emei beckon in joy.
Peerless they are in charm and elegance;
No need to cross the seas for the Land of Immortals.

Soaring 10,171 ft (3100 m) into the clouds in Emei County, Sichuan, this mountain was a sacred Taoist center as early as the Eastern Han dynasty (AD 25–AD 220), but its temples were taken over and rededicated in the spread of Buddhism. Several hundred monasteries were scattered around its lower slopes in its heyday, but now only a few remain. East of the main peak of Emei Mountain, and below Double Dragon Mountain, only three of the original seven buildings of this Jin dynasty monastery still stand today. And these that are still there were renovated in the reign of the Ming ruler Wanli. The most significant ones are Baoguo at the foot of the mountain, Wannian on its middle slope and Jinding at its summit.

Wannian monastery possesses rare Buddhist sutras written on the leaves of the Beiduoluo (Pattra) tree, as well as a 62-ton bronze sculpture of a Bodhisattva riding a six tusked elephant.

Since the Tang dynasty, Emei Mountain has been one of the four great Buddhist mountains of China.

Jiuzhai Valley

Surrounded by snowcapped mountains, this beauty spot in Jiuzhaigou County on the border of Sichuan and Gansu features dense forests, a total of 108 high-mountain lakes, one of China's most dramatic waterfalls, series of narrow conic karst land forms and unique wildlife. Its name refers to nine local villages, all inhabited by Tibetans.

The Shuzheng Waterfall is the spectacular spot of Jiuzhai Valley. Tumbling and dashing down a natural flight of stone steps, the Shuzheng Waterfall is about 200 ft (62 m) wide. It cascades some 50 ft (15 m) down to one of the scores of terraced lakes below. Not surprisingly, the local Tibetans have given the falls and their surrounding wooded lakes the name "fairyland."

Jiuzhai Valley, abundant with bamboo, is also a main habitat of the giant panda, China's most unique and most endangered native animal and symbol of the World Wildlife Fund. In the summer the pandas move up into the cooler mountain areas, where Tibetan tribespeople operate ingenious bamboo watermills in a rustic form of hydroelectric power. In the winter, the "bear cats," as the Chinese call them, return to the valleys and are known to scavenge village gardens and rubbish dumps for food.

The lakes in Jiuzhai Valley are so clear on a fine, still day that the rocky beds and underwater vegetation can be seen—giving them the names of Five-colored Lakes, Peacock Lake and Five-Flower Sea. It is regarded as one of the best tour resorts in China.

Huanglong Gully

Huanglong Scenic Area is located in Songpan County of Aba Tibetan-Qiang Autonomous Prefecture in the northwest of Sichuan Province. The scenic area covers 1,340 sq. km, with a core area of 700 sq. km. It is to the northeast of Xuebaoding, the main peak of Minshan Mountain. The comprehensive area includes Huanglong Valley, Danyun Gorge, Muni Valley, Xuebaoding, Xueshanliang, Hongxin (Red Heart) Crag, and Western Valley. You can find large open karst landscapes as well as other natural scenery. Folk customs of ethnic groups here are also interesting. Karst landscapes of Huanglong Valley, a typical representative of this kind in the world, are immense in scope and well-preserved. It is one of the first state-level scenic areas in China.

Danyun Gorge, Western Valley and Longdishui (Dragon Dripping Water) are the most attractive of the area. The dark forest covers both sides of the deep gorges, waterfalls tearing through grotesque stones and thundering down into the unknown world here. These strange stones, precipitous peaks, flowers and birds, insects and fish, clouds and red leaves can come together to make a natural scroll of a Chinese painting of mountains and waters.

Many ethnic minorities live in Huanglong, the local Tibetan, Qiang and Hui peoples. One can experience the folk customs of groups like Tibetan and Qiang with learning their Guozhuang dance, tasting their ghee tea and visiting their White Pagoda Temple.

Huanglong has the largest and most well-preserved open karst landscape in the world. Ponds, rivers and caves made from the karst form the large exposed pale yellow calcareous deposits that resemble a golden dragon from a bird's-eye view.

Huanglong is a gigantic gene bank with its primitive ecosystem. The area is like a natural oxygen bar due to the rich and abundant content of this element. Current statistics show that there are nearly 1,700 species of animals and plants, including pandas, golden hair monkeys, Chinese caterpillar fungus, Frillaria thunbergli and mushrooms.

Xueshanliang's (Snow Ridge) towering snow peak, precipitous cliffs and sea of clouds comprise a spectacular landscape.

Xuebaoding (Snow Peak), 5,588 m above sea level, is the main peak of Minshan mountain and looks like a jade pyramid—divine, noble and solemn. Around the peak are hundreds of mountain lakes and dozens of glaciers.

Red Heart Crag is a great mountain, where many clear lakes scatter around it. It is named after the dark rocks with a red heart-shaped patch on the mountain cliff. Under the sunshine, the Red Heart Crag turns golden, and the "heart" is mirrored in the lakes, projecting a fairyland-like scene.

The Huanglong Colored Ponds are the largest, and the most complete and unique karst landscape in the world, demonstrating the mastermind of nature.

Hailuogou

Hailuogou lies in the southeast of Ganzi Tibetan Autonomous Prefecture of Sichuan Province, east slope of Mount Gongga and is a skyscraping mountain in the east of Qinghai-Tibet Plateau. Hailuogou Scenic Area is a low altitude modern oceanic glacier, a complete virgin forest as well as an integrative scenic area consisting of boiling, hot, and cold springs in Asia. Furthermore, it is the nearest to metropolis, Chengdu and easy to reach. Hailuogou glacier is also called No.1 Glacier considering its length and large scope. It is 14.7 km long, the longest of the 71 glaciers in Mount Gongga, occupying an area of 16 sq. km with the highest height of 6750 m and lowest 2850 m. Basin, icefall, and glacier tongue run lengthwise, forming three continuous steps. The basin is the gestation place of glacier. The icefall, which is 500 m to 1100 m wide and 1080 m high is the highest and grandest icefall in China. The glacier tongue extends 6 km into the forest, forming a special convergence of forest and glacier.

The movement of Hailuogou Glacier is very active, forming a glacier circular arch, ice cavern, glacial staircase, ice gate and ice lake, which are as glittering and translucent as jade and crystal.

Hanas Lake

Much of the northwest of China remains a mystery. One of the jewels of the area is Hanas Lake, known only in the last 30 years to the outside world. It lies in the vast unspoiled frost on Altay Mountain (or gold mountain), in northern Xinjiang. Like many of the lakes and rivers in the region, it is formed from melted snow and is known as the most beautiful spot in the Uygur autonomous region, with a landscape said to match Switzerland. In fact, the word "hanas" in Mongolian means "beautiful, rich and mysterious." The mirror-flat mountain lake is famous for its changing color, dependent on vantage point, and ever-changing weather, winning Hanas Lake the title "the lake of changing colors." Surrounding the lake, a 2100-sq.mi. (5500-sq.km) nature reserve is rich in animal and plant resources. The mystery of a legendary "lake monster" adds more to the attraction of this serene and secluded area, where one can enjoy all kinds of activities, such as trekking, horseback riding, fishing, river valley drifting and camping.

The forested hillsides, Fairy Lake and hot springs constitute the amazing scenery of Hanas.

Potala Palace

This massive fortified palace and monastery, the "Vatican" of Tibetan Buddhism, looms across the crest of the Red Hill to the northeast of Lhasa. Construction of the palace began in the 7th century when the Prince of Tubo, Songsten Gampo, built what was then known as the Red Roofed Palace in honor of his Chinese consort, Princess Wencheng.

In 1642 the fifth Dalai Lama rebuilt the entire complex—pressing 7000 slaves into what turned out to be a full 50 years of work—as the seat of Tibetan Buddhism and government. Since then, Potala has comprised two main sections, known as the Red and White Palaces, with the White Palace housing vast courts of priests and monks and the Red Palace containing shrines, libraries and halls of worship. The buildings at the foot of the hill include administrative offices, workshops, a printing press and a prison.

Every year thousands of visitors have filed through the Potala since Tibet was reopened to foreigners in 1980, to view the magnificent apartment and such décor and relics as the wands, lined with tiger fur, that are the symbol of absolute authority; the predominant red and gold decoration of the rooms and their many priceless tapestries, carpets, murals and sculptures of Buddha and Bodhisattvas; the intricate carvings of the screens and furnishings and the vivid splashes of color from the woven and embroidered pillar rugs.

The White Palace on the top of Potala enjoys abundant sunlight through its spacious windows.

As a palace-castle complex, Potala is as security-conscious as it is sacred. Walls of enormous granite blocks protect it, along with a number of fortresses. As an added precaution, the walls are said to be reinforced with copper that strengthen them against earthquakes.

Nam Co

On the northern Tibetan Plateau, there are at least thirty-five lakes occupying an area of over 39 sq. mi. (100 sq. km). Among the largest is Nam Co, or Heavenly Lake. In summer, its surface is a bright sapphire blue and reflects the surrounding flowers. Nam Co is one of the four holiest lakes in Tibet. It is regularly visited by thousands of Buddhist pilgrims from Tibet and elsewhere. Pilgrims perform the required circuit of the lake and worship at the four monasteries situated on each side of the lake. Five small islands on the lake are believed to be an incarnation of the Buddha of the Five Directions, which makes Nam Co religious and drives pilgrims to make the long and difficult trip to the lake on foot. The five islands are covered with oddly shaped stones.

Surrounded by snowcapped peaks, Nam Co is the highest saltwater lake in the world at 15,000 ft (4700 m) above sea level.

Mount Qomolangma

Himalaya Range is the highest mountain range on earth and yet one of the youngest. It boasts 1471 peaks, 229 of which are more than 22,960 ft (7000 m) above the sea level. Mount Qomolangma, the mightiest mountain in the world at 29,029 ft (8848 m), is called Everest by Westerners who see it as a supreme test of courage and endurance and is regarded as the Goddess of the Snow Mountains by Tibetans, who venerate it for its beauty and grandeur. Over the centuries they have built palaces and gardens around its lower slopes —and a lamasery called Rongbu, which has the distinction of being the loftiest religious institution in the world.

Everest, or Qomolangma, is often shrouded by clouds and mist, which the Tibetan say is the "veil of the Holy Mother." For Western expeditions, these swirling mists are one of Everest's terrors, along with hurricane-force winds and storms that suddenly lash the snow and ice-covered slopes, the bitter temperatures (normally between 66 °C and 76 °C below zero), the lack of oxygen on the upper precipices and summit itself, which is little more than a precarious ridge about 3ft (1 m) wide and 39 ft (12 m) long—a tiny pinhead at the very roof of the world.

On the Tibetan side of Mount Qomolangma, there are 217 glaciers and one vast stretch of the slopes, between 18,710 ft (5700 m) and 21,982 ft (6700 m), which is literally a forest of ice. Its "trees" are huge columns and towers of frozen runoff.

Qomolangma is often shrouded by the "veil of the Holy Mother."

THE CENTRAL REGION

This region covers Shandong, Henan, Anhui, Jiangsu, Hubei, Hunan, Zhejiang and Jiangxi provinces, as well as Shanghai Municipality; the Yangtze, the nation's mightiest river which links the main waters and tributary system of the area—and, in many respects, can be called both the physical and emotional heartland of China.

In the northern part of this region, the Yellow River follows a path that slopes to the east as it cuts through the loess plateau and then curves through the Central Plain to empty into the Bo Sea. On its way, the river deposits vast quantities of alluvial soil, a process that gave birth to agricultural settlement along its banks 5000 to 6000 years ago, but has also given the river itself the name China's Sorrow. In areas near its estuary, the alluvial deposits are so heavy that the river's bed has risen many yards above the level of the surrounding land. Despite a complex system of dykes, established over the centuries to check and tame the river's course, occasional tremendous flooding has cost thousands of lives.

Another main artery in the southern part is the Yangtze River, 3900 mi. (6300 km) long and the world's third longest river after the Amazon and the Nile. Its complicated spider web of waterways knits together a territory that encompasses

the warm, temperate and semi-tropical provinces of Hubei, Hunan, Jiangxi, Anhui, Jiangsu and Zhejiang, all of which are rich agricultural areas producing most of the country's staple and "cash" crops, such as rice, cotton, silk, tobacco, peanuts, soybeans and tea, which in only three centuries has become the world's leading stimulative beverage.

With such an abundance of water—the Yangtze's network and most of China's 370 large lakes—the region also produces vast quantities of freshwater fish, and the Zhoushan Archipelago off Zhejiang Province reaches into China's richest offshore fishing ground. Shanghai lies just south of the Yangtze Delta, where the huge river meets the East China Sea. With about 19 million people, China's late-developing center of industry, finance, shipping and intellect is now a metropolis ranking in population with Greater Los Angeles.

The entire region is noted for its natural landscapes and dramatic beauty, ranging from deep gorges carved through the hills by the Yangtze; two famous sacred Buddhist mountains —Jiuhua in Anhui and Putuo in Zhejiang; the Province of a Thousand Lakes, Hubei; and the Yellow Mountain in southern Anhui, the area renowned for its pine forests, dramatic rock formations, "clouds seas" and hot springs.

THE CENTRAL REGION

As the heartland of China, this region has held the key throughout history to the domination of the entire empire. Its famous cities were first developed more than 3000 years ago. The region's wealth was the ultimate target of constant tribal military pressure from the north. Since the Eastern Jin dynasty (AD 317–AD 420), when the Chinese capital was moved to Nanjing, and later when the Song emperors were forced to move south, the region has been China's cultural center and most coveted economic prize. Many great battles and power struggles took place here throughout history.

Qufu

It is due to the influence of Confucius (551 BC–479 BC), the great philosopher, politician and educator of ancient China, in the 2,500-year history of China, that the Temple and Confucius Grave and the Confucius Residence, situated in Qufu City, the hometown of Confucius, enjoy great prestige.

The Temple of Confucius in Qufu is the oldest, largest and most architecturally representative. It houses over 1,000 steles dated from 149 BC to 1949. They are not only precious resources for the study of the politics, philosophy and culture of various dynasties, the history of the Temple, but also the treasure of Chinese calligraphy.

Forest of Confucius probably the most significant historic site in China, is where Confucius and his descendants were buried. It lies about a mile (1.5 km) north of Qufu City and boasts an ornate roofed gateway leading to the Forest of Confucius as well as a huge grove of 20,000 old and rare trees, some of which, it is claimed, were planted by Confucian disciples over the centuries.

After the death of Confucius, his disciples guarded the tomb for three years before leaving. The grave itself has the burial spot of Confucius's son to its east and that of his grandson to the south, conforming to the traditional burial pattern of "carrying the son and grandson," which indicates a flourishing population and continuing family line.

Each dynasty has contributed some of the finest artworks of its period as furnishings and decoration for the Confucius Residence and Temple.

Since Confucius set the ethical guidelines of Chinese society more than two millennia ago, successive dynasties have paid tribute to him and his descendants by bestowing honorary nobility on them, maintaining, and expanding the master's residence. The present Confucius Residence, as it is called, was built in the Song dynasty between 1038 and 1039 and has burgeoned in the centuries since then to conclude 460 buildings, including halls, clambers and living quarters.

On the stone tablet in front of the tomb are seal script style carved characters, which translate to "Tomb of The Greatest, Holiest, King of Culture."

Longmen Caves

The third of the three greatest Buddhist grottoes in China, these caves were dug around the year AD 493 on the bank of the Yi River, south of Luoyang City in Henan. Since then, the cliff has been literally honey-combed with grottoes—over 2000 of them containing 100,000 sculptured images, 40 stone towers and 3600 stone carvings and inscribed stelae and plaques. These stelae include 30 that feature a variety of styles of calligraphy known as the Twenty Types at Longmen.

At the southern end of Longmen, there is a temple named Fengxian. Its construction began in 672 during the reign of the Tang emperor, Gaozong, and it took four years to complete this, the largest of the open-air grottoes at Longmen. A donation from the Empress Wu helped the project along. The huge cavern, 115 ft (35 m) long and 98 ft (30 m) wide, features nine large Buddha statues, the tallest one standing nearly 59 ft (18 m) high. It has pronounced Han Chinese Buddha features, with long drooping ears and expressive eyes, and its robes are voluminous. In the north wall of the cave, there are statues of a Heavenly Guard and a strongman, both well-preserved. The guard supports a pagoda in the palm of its hand, and one of its feet rests heavily on a demon.

The Longmen caves feature sculptures of emperors, princes and nobles of those times alongside the Buddhas.

Most of the caves date back to the Northern Wei (AD 386–AD 534).

Yellow Mountain

Legend has it that the Yellow Emperor once tried to distill the Elixir of Life on this magnificent mountain between She and Taiping counties in Anhui. A Pailou (entrance arch) announces the area, the beauty of which has been celebrated for centuries.

Yellow Mountain's main peaks all rise over 5900 ft (1800 m). The sheer-cliffed peak, on which stands a solitary rock called Feilaishi or Flown Here Rock is one of the favorite places with a panoramic view of the scenic area.

Rearing in petrified waves towards the sky, Yuping (Jade Screen) Peak is another dramatic aspect of the Yellow Mountain area. It looms between Lianhua (Lotus Blossom) and Tiandu (Heavenly Capital) peaks and is close to the range's hot springs. It also features the Yuping Lodge, a well-positioned resting place for the weary climbers, which is said to stand where a monk, Pumen, dreamed of the Bodhisattva Majusri in the year 1614 and erected a shrine to commemorate the vision. At 5512 ft (1680 m), the entire peak is granite and was obviously created by some cataclysmic eruption hundreds of millions of years ago. This explains why both the ascent and descent are treacherous. Ways are steep, and one of the most dangerous points is the Xiaoxinpo (Be Careful Slope), which has a sheer wall on one side and overlooks a deep ravine on the other. Nearby lies the pretty, high-altitude Yuping Sky Lake.

Yellow Mountain is noted for its forests of pines, two lakes, three waterfalls, 24 streams, 72 peaks, hot spring, and its "sea of clouds."

The great Ming dynasty traveler Xu Xiake paid Yellow Mountain the warmest of all tributes when he wrote: "Having returned from the Five Sacred Mountains, one does not want to look at ordinary mountains; having returned from Yellow Mountain, one does not want to look at the Five Sacred Mountains."

Hong Village and Xidi Village

In the year 2000, two well-preserved villages in the southeast of Anhui Province were listed as World Cultural Heritage Sites. These beautiful villages, with many houses built 300–400 years ago, are tucked in a green, hilly area of Anhui. Xidi Village has the oldest houses, some dating back more than 400 years. An astounding number of houses, 122 in all, share elaborately shaped eaves and courtyards paved with dark-grey flag-stones or closely spaced pebbles in traditional designs. Seen from above, this small village of tightly spaced houses resembles a ship sailing the green hills of the area.

Hong villagers, on the other hand, claim that their village is as strong as an ox. A hike into the surrounding hills to view Hong Village from above reveals the resemblance to an ox resting on its side by a river after hard labor. The Chinese delight in finding resemblances to nature in their man-made creations, and in this lovely example the Hong Village entrance is the ox's head, and the trees there have been called the horns of the ox's head. The comparisons to an ox continue and include the bridges like hooves, and the body being the hundreds of closely spaced houses. The water around the village also fits the picture, with the river flowing alongside the village being the ox tail; a pond shaped like the stomach, and the intestines the network of the ditches essential to supply fresh water to every household.

Xidi and Hong villages have long been admired by visitors and scholars of Chinese domestic architecture, but it was not until 2000 when these Chinese ancient houses were put on a prestigious worldwide preservation list.

Slender West Lake

Slender West Lake in Yangzhou, Jiangsu Province, is in the long narrow shape. Moreover, it is regarded as beautiful as the West Lake in Hangzhou. Hence, the name conveys all the meanings. Its best feature is that all the gardens along the meandering lake have a distinctive style, separately constructed but harmoniously blending with towers in neighbouring courtyards and pink apricots hanging over walls mirrored in the water like paintings. Although "slender," the landscape is serene and graceful.

Five beautiful yellow-glazed tiled pavilions stand on a 15-arched bridge in Slender West Lake, built by a salt merchant in 1757 to commemorate a visit by the Qing emperor Qianlong, is one of the main attractions. It is also called Lotus Blossom Bridge because it was built on a bed of lotus plants, and for many years it has been a popular spot for one of the favorite traditional pastimes of the Chinese, viewing the moon and its reflection on still waters. The White Pagoda stands within the nearby Lianxing Monastery and is a copy of the White Pagoda in Beijing's Beihai Park. It is said that the salt merchant had it built in one single night to impress the visiting emperor—a story that is taken with a grain of salt.

Originally, this scenic area was a group of private gardens.

Suzhou Gardens

Suzhou is one of the oldest cities on the lower reaches of the Yangtze River and on the shores of Tai Lake in the province of Jiangsu. Tai Lake, four fifths of which is in the territory of Suzhou, is one of the four largest fresh lakes in China.

Large area of the city is covered by water, including a vast number of ponds and streams. The Beijing-Hangzhou Grand Canal from north to south cuts the city.

Suzhou is an ancient city with a 2500 years' history. Since the Song dynasty (AD 960–1279), Suzhou has been an important center for China's silk industry. It's "a very great and noble city ... It has 1600 stone bridges under which a galley may pass." (Marco Polo) Strolling on the streets, you can feel the unique charm of this landscape left by its long history.

The classic gardens full of poetic and artistic conception of the traditional Chinese freehand brushwork paintings are made through the elaborate arrangement of rocks, water, vegetation, and deliberate layout of the buildings. Classical gardens in Suzhou were added to the list of the UNESCO World Heritage Sites in 1997 and 2000. At present more than 60 gardens are kept intact in Suzhou. Among those gardens, Master-of-Nets Garden, West Garden, Humble Administrator's Garden, the Lion Forest Garden, the Couple's Garden Retreat, Lingering Garden and the Garden of Cultivation are well-known.

The garden's overall appearance, though man-made, appears to be formed by nature.

The unique character of
Suzhou is embodied by its
classic gardens.

Three Gorges

As the name indicates, the so-called three Gorges is consisted of three gorges located in the upper reaches of the Yangtze River. Renowned for the magnificent landscapes, three Gorges are called the "picture corridor" of mountain and river.

Qutang Gorge is the shortest and most dramatic of Three Gorges. Its mouth is very narrow, less than 328 ft (100 m) across, with steep walls on both sides, and the Tang dynasty poet Bai Juyi, came up with this description: "The banks are like two screens kept ajar, through which the sky peeks." Guarding the mouth of the gorge are two mountains—Chijia Mountain on the left and Bai Yan Mountain (White Salt Mountain) on the right.

In a steep wall on the north bank, there are a number of neatly carved rectangular caves, which are believed to have contained the remains of nobles of the Warring States period (475 BC–221 BC). Nine "hanging coffins" have been found, containing human bones and bronze swords. The tiny tombs are similar to those of the Toraja mountain tribe in South Sulawesi, Indonesia.

Wu Gorge is the most picturesque of the Three, a scenic picture gallery cutting more than 25 mi. (40 km) through the main ridge of Wu Mountain. Xu Rulong of the Qin dynasty became enthusiastic about the scene, writing, "As I put out my boat in the Wu Gorge my heart is with the twelve peaks"—referring to the 12 mountain

In the past, this stretch of water was treacherous when the river levels were low and its rocks were exposed like jagged teeth. When the Yangtze was swollen and the rocks were submerged, there was an even greater danger to the hulls of river crafts. This hazard is gone after the damming of the river in Yichang, Hubei Province.

summits that range around the narrow waterway. Beneath on particular peak, Jixian (Gathering Immortals), the scene is described with crushing simplicity in an inscription that reads, "Multiple-Cliffs-and-Piled-Up-Hills Wu Gorge."

Spanning a distance of 44 mi. (70 km) between Sichuan and Hubei Provinces, the Xiling Gorge is the longest of the three, and it was once the most dangerous before Gezhouba Dam was built. There used to be not only narrow passages bristling with half-submerged rocks but a series of severe rapids too, including the perilous Kongling Rapids, which a local folk song had described as the "demon's gate."

Fenghuang City

In western Hunan, the small town called Fenghuang—or Phoenix City—is a wonderful place to see the Miao, one of China's best-known ethnic minorities. Legend, history, Miao architecture and customs are all part of a visit. There are two very different stories for the name of the town. Legend has it that a pair of phoenixes was once spotted in the area, but, once noticed, they flew away. A more historical account ignores the idea of the mythical birds altogether and tells of the town growing from a Han military camp situated there to quell the Miao. Many of the soldiers stayed, and now the town is inhabited by both the Miao and the Han Chinese. Visitors can take a ride in the slim wooden boats of the Miao. The enticing smell of ginger candy wafts into the streets from the many candy workshops. Once a year, during the time the rest of China celebrates the Dragon Boat Festival, the local people have their own wild and exciting day, called Duck Chasing. Thousands of ducks specially gathered for this amazing free-for-all are released into the river. A gripping chase follows, and whoever catches the ducks keeps them!

The peculiar Miao building style called hanging attic is used in houses that line the riverbank. Although the foundations look precarious, the houses using traditional methods are safe, sturdy homes and have sheltered the Miao for many decades.

Shen Congwen, one of China's great 20th century writers, grew up in Fenghuang City, where his father was in the military. He wrote many novels, and one of his most popular presents a vivid picture of the Miao life, where the natives still wear ethnic costume and preserve their folk songs.

Zhangjiajie

Zhangjiajie may refer to the city that used to be called Dayong, as well as the Zhangjiajie National Forest Park, the first national park in China established in 1982. Formerly known as Green Cliff Mountain, noted for its picturesque or bizarre rock formations, Zhangjiajie is a group of 2000 mountain peaks at the junction of three counties in Hunan Province. Legend and imagination have given the peaks various names, such as Golden Whip Boulder, in memory of an incident in which the first emperor of Qin is said to have lost a whip there. Other peaks are known as Three Sisters, Rooster Cliff, or Monkeys-Storming-Heavenly-Palace Peak, depending on their shapes.

Zhangjiajie is one of the four spots of a greater scenic area called Wulingyuan, the other three being Yangjiajie, Suoxiyu and Tianzi Mountain. All four cover a total area of close to 300 sq. mi. (500 sq. km).

West Lake

The West Lake was called Golden Cow Lake before the Song dynasty because a golden cow was said to materialize on its waters whenever a sage or holy man passed by. The poet Su Shi (Dongpo) compared the lake with the famous beauty Xi Shi, writing that like the courtesan, "it is attractive with make-up or without." The lake site used to be a shallow bay connected to the Qiantang River but was gradually sealed off by alluvial deposit, and dredging and landscaping did the rest.

This oval-shaped lake has an area of about 2.3 sq. mi. (6 sq. km) and a circumference of 9.3 mi. (15 km). The average depth of the lake is about 5 ft (1.5 m), with the deepest part being only 9 ft (2.8 m) and the shallowest spot less than 3.3 ft (1 m).

The city of Hangzhou stands on its eastern shore. On the gentle slopes of the hills surrounding the three sides of the lake are large gardens displaying a variety of flora: peach blossom in spring, lily in summer, osmanthus in autumn and plum blossom in winter. The hills are dotted with pavilions, pagodas, grottoes, mansions and streams.

The lake also adds its beauty and mystique to the Ten Beautiful Sites of Hangzhou—Autumn Moon over the Smooth Lake, Spring Dawn over the Su Bridge, Snow over the Broken Bridge, Dusk at the Thunder Peak Pagoda, Evening Bell from Nanping, Waving Lotuses on a Garden Pond, Golden Carp in Huagang, Listening to the Nightingales under Willows on Lakeside, Moon Reflected on the Three Ponds and Double Peaks Piercing the Clouds.

Hangzhou and its West Lake have been immortalized by countless poets and artists.

Lu Mountain

This, one of China's most delightful mountains, rears to the south of Jiujiang City and overlooks the Yangtze River. Its name Lu means lodge, and legend says it was where seven brothers named Kuang built a lodge in the time of the Zhou dynasty (c.1046 BC –c.221 BC). Legend also has it that the great healer, Dong Feng, one of the noted mountain shamans of early Chinese history, made his home at the foot of the mountain. He is said to have refused payment for his services and usually asked his patients to plant five apricot trees when they recovered. In the time of the Eastern Han dynasty, more than 380 monasteries existed on the mountain's slopes, a few of which still stand after centuries of care and renovation.

The ever-changing mist enables the mountain to pose diversely and shrouds the mountain all the year round. Just as Su Shi, a well-known poet of Song dynasty, once pointed out in one of his poems, the failure to get the real looks of the mountain only results in the fact that you are right in the midst of it. Although a clear view of the mountain is hided, the sea of clouds presents a feeling of fairyland.

Lu Mountain's "sea of clouds" is a celebrated tourist attraction, as are its many peaks, caves, pools and waterfalls.

Wuyuan

Situated northeast of Jiangxi Province near the borders of Anhui and Zhejiang, Wuyuan County is endowed with that special beauty so admired in Chinese landscape painting. Its rolling mountains, crystal-clear creeks, bamboo forests, strange rock formations, caves, tea plantations and ancient trees are the perfect inspiration for the painter and poet, and yet it has been largely overshadowed as a destination by the nearby Yellow and Lu mountains. The other attraction in the area for visitors from all over the world is the famous porcelain capital Jingdezhen.

Visitors are entranced by Wuyuan County's villages and countryside, claimed to be the finest in China.

As for history, Wuyuan County boasts some of the best preserved ancient architecture from the Ming and Qing dynasties. It even boasts an 800-year-old covered Rainbow Bridge of the Song dynasty. Scholarship has had a long tradition also. Wuyuan has produced an amazing number of scholars who passed the imperial court exams, 550 in all. Probably the best know is Zhu Xi, a late Song dynasty scholar, who was the co-founder for the Cheng-Zhu Confucian School and who wrote what was later accepted as the standard interpretation of Confucian learning in the imperial examinations.

In ancient times Wuyuan was counted as part of Anhui's Huizhou Prefecture and was known for being the home of one of the three most influential merchant groups in China, called the Hui merchants.

Wuyuan, with its idyllic scenery, has been a favorite for poets and writers over the ages. Its seclusion kept it a hidden secret until recently when vacationers, tired of the usual tourist destinations, began to look for new places with historical interest as well as natural beauty.

The Bund in Shanghai

For over a century has been regarded as a symbol of Shanghai, the Bund shows off city's outstanding buildings that line the Huangpu River, showcasing different architectural styles including Gothic, Baroque, Romanesque, Classicism and the Renaissance. It stretches one mile along the bank of the Huangpu River. Traditionally, the Bund begins at Yan'an Road in the south and ends at Waibaidu Bridge in the north, which crosses the Suzhou Creek. A row of 52 unique buildings integrating the Oriental and Occidental architectural styles, generally is known as a museum of "buildings in multinational styles of architecture." Nowadays the Bund is one of the city's chic places, which world-class luxury brands can be found. It's a favorite haunt for fashion lovers and the rich and famous people.

At night, floodlights illuminate the grand structures of the Bund to highlight their magnificent architectural styles.

THE SOUTHERN REGION

The southern region of China, which covers the provinces of Yunnan, Guizhou, Guangdong, Guangxi Zhuang Autonomous Region, Fujian, Taiwan, and Hong Kong and Macau special administrative regions, is not noted for its role as a vanguard in Chinese history. However, it was one of the first areas of China to trade with the outside world and was the scene of a bitter 19th century struggle with the British Empire that ultimately brought the age-old dynastic tradition to an end. It was the power struggle in the Opium Wars, from 1839 to 1842 and 1856 to 1860, that centered on the thriving trading concession at Guangzhou (Canton). After the British Navy defeated China's imperial war junks, the British obtained control over the island of Hong Kong and a portion of the mainland territory as a colony. This opened the way for an international "carve-up" of Chinese sovereignty that a weakened, antiquated Qing dynasty could not effectively resist.

Physically, the region is divided into the highlands of Yunnan and Guizhou and the lowland areas of the other provinces. These in turn are dotted with abrupt, bizarrely shaped towers and cones of limestone, giving Guilin its unique and long-renowned beauty, and poets and painters a fountainhead of inspiration. Fast-flowing rivers crisscross the region, gouging deep gorges in the karst terrain—as deep as 10,000 ft (3000 m) in the highland areas—and the landscape also features massive caves, underground rivers, "stone forests" and red sandstone terraces. The climate ranges from subtropical to tropical, and is influenced along the coastal areas by both the monsoon and the dreaded typhoon —powerful hurricane-force anticyclones that boil up out of the Pacific, south of the Philippines and surge north to thrash themselves, one after the other, on the south China coast.

Though it doesn't play an important role in Chinese history, the legacy of Fujian province's political importance between the 8th and 13th centuries also can be found in this region. Perhaps, the greatest of the region's legacies is the role it played for centuries as a refuge for scholar mandarins who had lost favor in the imperial courts.

The region is also famous for being a flashpoint of resistance, the last and greatest of these being the Republican Campaign (1911) against the Manchu ruler led by the sons and daughters of southern merchants and officials. Those in the resistance, like the region itself, had become more modernized and therefore more progressive in thought than China's northern areas through contact with foreign traders, teachers and missionaries.

Shangri-La

Shangri-La is located in the heart of the Hengduan Mountain Range, which is rich with many natural attractions, such as Bita Lake Nature Preserve, Napa Lake White Water Terrace, Haba Snow Mountain, Meili Snow Mountain. Shangri-La has a number of ethnic groups besides the Tibetan people. The smaller groups include Naxis, the Lisus and the Yis. Their exotic customs and ancient way of life add much charm to the area's natural beauty. A vast system of rivers traverses the snow-covered mountains and deep valleys. Typical of the area is the Birang Valley, tucked deep in the mountains. The 6-mi. (10-km) long valley is surrounded by sheer cliffs and at places is over 6000 ft (2000 m) deep along a narrow valley, very much like the one described in *Lost Horizon*. The deep valleys are flanked by some of the highest mountain peaks in the world. Kagebo Peak, known as the Chief of the Eight Sacred Peaks, soars 22,114 ft (6740 m), still destined to be conquered by mankind.

Long known as Zhongdian, this mountainous region in northwestern Yunnan Province was renamed Shangri-La in 2001 after the paradise of peaceful tranquility of snowy mountains, grasslands, Tibetan people and red soil plateaus, vividly described by the British writer James Hilton in his novel *Lost Horizon*. Shangri-La is a Tibetan word that means "land of sacredness and peace."

This area once served as a major caravan stop on the ancient tea trade routes between India, South China and Burma.

Meili Snow Mountain

Meili Snow Mountain has long been famous for its main peak, Kagebo Peak, which is 21,221 ft (6,470 m) above sea level, the highest in Yunnan.

The snow-capped Meili is distinctly different in the four seasons. Between the foot and the summit, there are several systems of plant distributions, varying from the tropical zone to the Tundra zone. The snowline divides two sharply different scenes. Above it, there are steep snow-capped peaks admist cloud and mist, and below are evergreen vegetation and flowers in full bloom.

The 13 peaks of the Meili are more than 6000 m above the sea level, which are called the Prince 13 peaks. Mount Kagebo, the main peak of the Meili Snow Mountain is a holy place of pilgrimage for Tibetan Buddhists. For local Tibetans, Mount Kagebo is the residence of their guardian deity. They protect the mountain from being scaled by man or else the god will leave, and disasters will arise. In the 1930s, the American scholar Joseph Rock ventured to the Meili Mountain. Attracted by the enchanting Mount Kagebo, he described it as the most beautiful snow mountain in the world. In late autumn and early winter every year, pilgrims from Tibet, Sichuan, Qinghai and Gansu travel hundreds of kilometers to pay homage to the sacred mountain. They prostrate their way around the holy mountain for one to two weeks. This is called "circumambulation" by local residents. Each Goat year in the Tibetan Calendar, the number of "circumambulators" increases a hundredfold.

Kagebo Peak is extolled as the "most beautiful mountain in the world." It means White Snow Mountain in Tibetan language and is surrounded by 13 lesser peaks, which are the subject of an enchanting tale.

Lijiang

The old town area in Lijiang probably has the greatest number of timber houses still in their original Naxi village setting in China. The cleverly engineered water system taps a clean water source high in the mountains above Lijiang, channeling streams to the town to bring water to the residents along each street and to the neighborhood pit wells designated for drinking water, vegetable washing and clothes washing. Each timber house is beautifully decorated with carvings. They are not built to delight the eye only. When a strong earthquake destroyed most masonry buildings of recent construction in Lijiang and killed 300 people in 1996, most of the timber houses of the Naxi withstood the quake with little damage. In tribute to the ingenious local Naxi architecture, the government decided to rebuild with timber structures. An evening stroll might allow the lucky visitors to watch a Naxi folk dance. There are opportunities to learn about the religious beliefs of the Naxi and to visit one of the tallest wooden pagodas in China, carved with Dongba scripture. Only the shamans of the Naxi are taught to read and write the more than 1000 Dongba pictographs. Lijiang has one of the tallest wooden pagodas in China.

High above Lijiang towers the Jade Dragon Snow Mountain, which is really a mountain range 22 mi. (35 km) long. The tallest of these breathtaking peaks is Shanzidou or Fan Peak at over 18360 ft (5596 m). Although difficult to climb, Fan Peak was finally scaled in 1963.

In Lijiang, visitors can wander the narrow cobblestone streets while admiring the Naxi-style timber houses.

Lugu Lake

High in an isolated area of the province of Yunnan, Lugu Lake is home to one of the few existing matriarchal societies. The remote land around the lake, located on a 900-ft-(300-m-) high plateau ringed with towering mountains, has protected the culture of the matriarchal Mosuo people, who are part of the Naxi ethnic minority group. The pristine waters of Lugu Lake vary from intense blue and turquoise to milky gray-white. The lake is rich in carp and many other species of fish, and visitors will see a native-style fishing boat plying the waters.

An elaborate system of courtship, including an exchange of tokens, begins a relationship between Mosuo men and women, and when by mutual consent love and affection exist, there is often an agreement witnessed and celebrated by the families of the couple. But the word marriage does not define their relationship, called "Axia;" instead the term "dear companion" serves the pair in this female-centered society. Men continue to live their entire lives at the home of their mother, visiting their "dear companion" each day. For the children of this relationship, the word father is not used. "Maternal uncle" defines this role in its place. Mosuo women are the leaders of the family, and goddess worship is practiced in this unusual mountain kingdom.

The mountainous area of Lugu Lake has been named the Female Kingdom by the Chinese for many years.

Yellow Fruit Tree Waterfall

Close to Rhinoceros Cave, this waterfall, the largest in China, spans a width of 98–131 ft (30–40 m) and thunders 197 ft (60 m) down into Rhinoceros Pool, a cascade almost equaling the size and power of Niagara Falls on the United States–Canadian border. The waterfall derived its name from the "yellow fruit tree" (tangerine) plantations found upstream of the River Baishui, which at this point in Guizhou's Zhenning County descends the hill slopes in nine steps, this waterfall being the highest and most dramatic.

A pavilion on the opposite cliff commands a full view of the cascade, and in a stalactite cave below, spectators can watch the magnificent downpour through three openings.

It is claimed that the roar of the falling water can be heard up to 3 mi. (5 km) away.

Yuanyang Terraced Fields

Yuanyang terraced fields lie within the Yuanyang county of Honghe Hani and Yi Autonomous Prefecture in Yunnan Province, on the south part of Ailao Mountain. They are majestic and extend through the whole of Honghe, Yuanyang, Lüchun and Jinping counties on the south bank of the Honghe River. Only within Yuanyang county does it cover an area of about 17,000 *mu* (a Chinese unit, one *mu* equals about 667 sq. m), which makes Yuanyang the core area of the Honghe Hani terraced fields.

The terraced fields consist of three main areas: Beida scenic area with 14,000 *mu* of stretching terraces, Laohuzui scenic area with 6,000 *mu*, and Duoyishu scenic area with about 10,000 *mu*. The numerous terraces among thick forests, amidst sea of clouds, achieve a picturesque scroll.

On the Ailao Mountain, thousands of terrace steps wind along the slopes, elevating into the unknown. After the autumn harvest, cold and clear water oozes into the fields, and everywhere shines golden in the morning and even in the evening. Sapphire blue and white clouds are projected onto the fields, and then all the colors seem to flow together. The light and color varies every second. It feels like being lost in a labyrinth being there. Sometimes, the clouds and mist roll above the distant mountain village, evoking the mystique of Shangri-La. When the spring comes, there is another picture, everything comes to life and there is hustle and bustle everywhere.

All the terraces are cut into slopes between 15 degrees and 75 degrees. For one slope, there can be 3,000 steps of terrace at most, which is rare in the world.

Li River

Fishermen on bamboo rafts, their lamps lit to attract shoals of fish, add to the fairyland effect of the Li River and its most scenic stretch between Guilin and Yangshuo. The men use tamed cormorants to make their catches. The Li River, a principal tributary of the River Gui, flows from Xing'an northwest of Guilin through to Yangshuo and then joins the West River after a distance of 272 mi. (437 km).

Its waters are varied. The Guilin-Yangshuo stretch is so placid that one can see the pebbles lying on the riverbed. Elsewhere, the rapids can be difficult to negotiate.

The numerous, rugged peaks on the two sides of the meandering river offer a feast to the river traveler's eye.

Yuan Mei, the Qing poet, marveled at the swift-changing scenery and made the following observation of the Li River tour, "One moment, you see the green peaks floating over your head; the next they glide under your boat."

Yangshuo

Certainly, the contrast of limestone and tropical green, and the hills and their surrounding flat paddy lands, is one scenic aspect of this karst landscape. The Li River winds through the hills like a green silk ribbon. The town of Yangshuo itself, at the end of a 50-mi. (80-km) boat cruise from Guilin City, is one of the most picturesque centers of the area and is surrounded by karst peaks that resemble ancient Chinese hats, galloping horses, a paintbrush and a five-fingered hand. All this, packed into a small town area, has inspired the following Tang dynasty saying: "The town walls encircle less than two *li* of space, but all the houses are hidden among ten thousand hills."

To the north of Yangshuo lies Xingping, which is reputed to have "the best of Yangshuo's landscape." There, fishing rafts crisscrossing the Li River against a dramatic backdrop of hills are a typical sight.

There is a well-known saying that goes, "The rivers and hills of Guilin are the most beautiful in China, and those of Yangshuo surpass Guilin's."

World's End in Hainan Island

Hainan, off the southernmost tip of China, is the second largest of the nation's 5000 or more islands. Covering an area of 12,352 sq. mi. (32,000 sq. km), the island is low-lying in the north and mountainous in the central region and south.

World's end, in Chinese Tianya Hajiao, is a somber-looking beach spot with its two huge boulders on the southern tip of Hainan Island. It was about as far as any Chinese official cared to go in ancient times. Even then, it meant shame to be exiled to "the end of the world." It reflected the view in those days that the civilized world ended on the borders of Chinese civilization. Today, riding on the swift changes in Haikou and Sanya, the two major cities on Hainan Island that have been dubbed "China's Hawaii," this quiet beach has become one of the busiest tourist destinations.

Most parts of the island are idyllic, lush forests and beautiful tropical beaches.

Hakka Earth Towers

In a long migration to the southern coastal area from war-ravaged northern China near the end of the Tang dynasty more than 1,000 years ago, a group of Hakka people, also known as the Jews of China, settled down in coastal Fujian Province. Their sense of insecurity brought them to several remote mountain valleys in Fujian. These northern migrants created one of the most unique architectures in Chinese history. What they built is known today as earth towers, a ring-shaped self-contained housing complex, resembling a circular fortress.

The tower itself is comparable to a Western-style castle whose sole entrance opens to a huge open-air central courtyard with views open to all the rooms built surrounding the yard. The tower can also take a variety of shapes: rectangular, semi-circular and square. A small earth tower rises up two stories and has one ring and more than twenty-one rooms. Bigger constructions can go as high as five stories, with multiple rings and as many as fifty-eight rooms. The inner rings are often shaped like a rice bowl, with the height of inner rings lower than the outside rings. The Hakka people use these rooms for multiple functions, as bathrooms, kitchens, family shrines, as well as schools, warehouses and theaters.

Earth towers spread mainly across three counties in Fujian Province: Yongding, Nanjing and Pinghe. The most renowned earth tower, the two-ringed Zhencheng Tower built in 1912, is in Yongding County.

For generations, these towers have shielded the Hakka people, their families and living quarters against invasion. Japanese pirates, who wreaked havoc along Chinese coastal provinces during the Ming dynasty in the 15th century, often skipped the Hakka earth tower areas in search of easier targets.

Xiamen Gulangyu

Gulangyu Island is located to the southwest of Xiamen City. Tourists can get there by steamship from Xiamen City in about 5 minutes. The delicate natural beauty, ancient relics, and the varied architecture contribute to the island's present fame. This island is on the list of China's National Scenic Spots and the top among the ten most-scenic areas of Fujian Province.

During the late Ming dynasty, the troops of national hero Zheng Chenggong were stationed here. After the Opium War in 1842, it became a common concession of 13 countries, including Great Britain, France and Japan. It was occupied by Japan from 1942 to 1945, the end year of the War of Resistance against Japan.

Gulangyu Island has about 20,000 permanent residents, and they all enjoy a comfortable, relaxing life. Only electric-powered vehicles are permitted on the island, so the air is free from the noise and pollution of combustion engines. Anyone here can feel like they were in heaven, breathing the clean air and appreciating the ever-present green trees and lovely flowers. With many classical and romantic European-style architectures, the island deserves the name of "Architecture Museum." It is also known as the "Cradle of Musicians" and "Island of Music."

The Island Ring Road, circling the island, allows one to fully enjoy all the sights of this small charming getaway.

Among the many scenic spots on the island, the most attractive are Sunlight Rock and the Shuzhuang Garden.

During the Ming dynasty (1368–1644), the Gulangyu was called "Yuanshazhou Island." The present name comes from its surrounding huge reef. When the tide comes in, the waves pound the reef and it sounds like someone beating a drum. Then the island came to be named "Gulang." *Gu* in Chinese means "drum," and *lang*, "waves."

Sun Moon Lake

Lying in Nantou County and covering more than 3 sq. mi. (7.5 sq. km), Sun Moon Lake is the largest natural lake in Taiwan. It takes its name from its shape—the northern half is round like the sun, and the southern section is crescent-shaped. It is a popular resort, with a summer temperature of about 22°C and a temperature in winter rarely falling below about 15°C. Sun Moon Lake is surrounded by green mountains, where the beauty of the lake can be found. The mountains that reach farther and farther away until they fade into the sky.

South of the lake there is a hill called Green Dragon, where several monasteries stand. One of them contains relics that are said to be those of the Tang dynasty monk Tripitaka.

The area around the Sun Moon Lake is home to the Shao tribe, one of aboriginal tribes in Taiwan. Between the "sun" and the "moon," there lies an island in the middle of the lake, which has long been a sacred place for the Shao people. Only the Shao people can be allowed to go there to worship their ancestors.

The view from the bank of the lake contains countless peaks rising up into the sky.

Hong Kong Victoria Harbor

Victoria Harbor, one of the world's busiest ports, is located between Hong Kong Island and Kowloon Peninsula. The most spectacular buildings around the harbor are the Bank of China Tower with 72 stories and the Central Plaza with 78 stories. The Bank of China's bamboo-like shape represents its pursuit for continued improvement. Kowloon, just across the harbor, is the location for many tourist hotels and all kinds of shopping.

The 10-minute famed Star Ferry ride offers panoramic views of Victoria Harbor with IFC Phase Ⅱ , the Bank of China and Hong Kong and Shanghai Bank buildings, and central Plaza on the Hong Kong side, and the HK Cultural Center, Peninsula Hotel, and Regent Hotel on the Kowloon side.

After dark, the whole city is a spectacular sight of glittering neon lights along the banks of Victoria Harbor. Victoria Peak, the highest point within Hong Kong that occupies the western part of the island, is the best location to view the luminous Victoria Harbor and the sea of lights twinkling in the streets.

Along the Victoria Harbor, shiny towers stand prominently on the Central District, which is Hong Kong's financial and economic hub.

Macau

A densely packed city of 450,000, where 70 percent of government revenue comes from the gambling industry today, Macau became the first European colony in Asia when in 1557 the Portuguese settled in the South China Sea to conduct the highly lucrative business of trade between Europe and the rest of Asia. The riches of Portugal's far-flung trading empire to the west brought spices, ivory, gold and highly coveted European technological inventions through this tiny settlement.

The Portuguese also brought along their specially trained missionaries. The Façade of Sao Paulo, now the only existing part of the church of Saint Paul, was the first church built in Macau in the early 17th century. The magnificent stone façade shows traces of the contributions of Portugal's Christian converts along its trading route, who were brought to Macau to help and may also have been sheltered there from the backlash against the church's activity in Asia.

The best way to get acquainted with Macau is through a walking tour of the historic beginning at Largo do Senado (Senate Square). This Senate Square is paved in black and white stone tiles in a swirling wave pattern typical of Portugal. Surrounding the square are beautifully restored colonial buildings painted in delightful pastels with white, used to pick out their wonderful baroque details. It is a great place to sit and watch the doings of a community that still uses its town square for local events, socializing and meeting friends.

Macau exemplifies the fascinating results of the meeting and blending of two very different cultures for nearly 450 years.